CREATIVE
Embroidery
& BEYOND

JENNY BILLINGHAM
SOPHIE TIMMS
THERESA WENSING

Brimming with creative inspiration, how-to projects, and useful information to enrich your everyday life, quarto.com is a favorite destination for those pursuing their interests and passions.

Photos on pages 6-21 © Shutterstock; text on pages 6-21 by Kelly Fletcher. Artwork and text on pages 22-71 © 2023 Jennifer Billingham; pages 72-107 © Theresa Wensing; pages 108-143 © 2023 Sophie Timms.

First published in 2023 by Walter Foster Publishing, an imprint of The Quarto Group. 100 Cummings Center, Suite 265D, Beverly, MA 01915, USA.
T (978) 282-9590 **F** (978) 283-2742 **www.quarto.com** • **www.walterfoster.com**

Contains content previously published from *Embroidery for Everyone* (becker&mayer!, 2021).

Walter Foster Publishing titles are also available at discount for retail, wholesale, promotional, and bulk purchase. For details, contact the Special Sales Manager by email at specialsales@quarto.com or by mail at The Quarto Group, Attn: Special Sales Manager, 100 Cummings Center, Suite 265D, Beverly, MA 01915, USA.

ISBN: 978-0-7603-8307-0

Digital edition published in 2023
eISBN: 978-0-7603-8308-7

Cover & layout design: Stacy Wakefield Forte
Copyedit: Caitlin Fultz
Proofread: Tracy Wilson

Printed in China
10 9 8 7 6 5

CREATIVE
Embroidery
& BEYOND

JENNY BILLINGHAM
SOPHIE TIMMS
THERESA WENSING

Table of Contents

step-by-step projects by

JENNY BILLINGHAM

Introduction

IF YOU'RE A BEGINNER, the trick to falling in love with embroidery is simply to enjoy doing it. Everyone starts somewhere, so go easy on yourself to begin with—the more embroidery you do, the better and quicker at it you'll get and the more you'll enjoy doing it. Start small if necessary and build up to bigger projects. Switch stitches if you prefer doing one over another. And use your favorite colors. If you like the challenge of diving in at the deep end, break your design up into segments so you feel a sense of achievement as you finish each one.

If you're a more experienced stitcher, you'll already be enjoying the benefits of hand embroidery, from improved eye-hand coordination and brain activity to reduced stress and anxiety levels.

Either way, embroidery is a great way to practice mindfulness. It's also a lovely way to spend time alone, whether for an afternoon or a week. While your hands are busy, listen to an audiobook or podcast, unwind or process your thoughts, relish learning something new, or simply keep boredom and negativity at bay if you're stuck at home.

Whatever your skill level, there are a few things that make it easier to embroider. They'll improve your skills and increase your sense of satisfaction and enjoyment. Feeling comfortable while stitching not only contributes to a better end result—it also allows you to stitch for longer stretches at a time. Try a few different places: a table, a couch, or an armchair. Your arms need to be able to move freely and it helps to have something to rest your hoop hand against while stitching, whether a tabletop or a plump cushion on your lap.

Good light—daylight or a suitable lamp—will reduce strain on your eyes and because you can see well, your stitching will automatically be easier and neater. Try to sit in a way that keeps the strain on your neck and back to a minimum. Remember to get up, shake out your hands and stretch every now and then. If you wear glasses, take your work with you to your next appointment and ask your optometrist for advice, as suitable lenses can be a big help. And if that's not enough, look for a craft magnifier (they often come as a package with craft lamps).

Most importantly, remember that hand embroidery is just that, embroidery done by hand—imperfections are part of the process and everyone's stitching will be unique to them. And if you have to unpick a little every now and then, or even begin a project over from scratch, so be it. Just get started, learn, experiment, and enjoy the process.

Tools & Materials

FABRIC

When choosing fabric, look for a smooth cotton that has a tight weave and isn't too thick. The thread colors used in this book's patterns are best suited to white or light color fabrics.

Backing your embroidery fabric is optional, but tacking a piece of cotton voile or finely woven muslin fabric to the back helps stabilize your stitching and gives you the option of starting (and ending) new threads with a small double stitch through the backing fabric only.

NEEDLES

Embroidery needle: Sometimes called crewel needles, embroidery needles have a long, oval eye that can hold numerous strands of thread. They come in various sizes and your thread should pull easily through the eye, but not so much so that it slips out while you're stitching.

Milliner/straw needle: Milliners are also known as straw needles. They are the same width from eye to tip and are suited to doing French and bullion knots as they pull easily through wraps of thread.

Use the embroidery needle for all the stitches in this book other than French knots, bullion knots, and pistil stitch. For those, use the milliner/straw needle.

HOOP

An embroidery hoop helps keep your fabric taut and stops your work from puckering as you stitch.

Place the inner hoop on a flat surface and lay your fabric over the top with the section of the design you're about to embroider in the center. Loosen the screw on the outer hoop just enough so it slips over the fabric and sandwiches it between the inner and outer hoops, and then tighten the screw. Grip your fabric on either side of the hoop and pull it taut (you want it drum tight), but take care not to distort the design when you do this. You may need to redo this last step a few times as you embroider, as the fabric might sag a bit in the hoop after stitching for a while.

Move your hoop around so you're able to work the stitches comfortably. Sometimes the embroidered stitches can become squashed or sink into the fabric. To fix this, pinch and lift stitches back into place using the nails of your thumb and forefinger, or slide your needle under the squashed sections and lift the stitches up again. You can avoid squashing knots and bullions by doing them last.

PATTERN TRANSFER TECHNIQUES

There are many ways to transfer printed patterns onto your fabric. Below are some of them.

Iron-on transfers: Iron-on transfers are printed using special ink that allows you to transfer designs onto fabric accurately using a hot iron. To use this technique, digitally scan the designs from the book and print onto iron-on transfer sheets. Remember to reverse the designs so they will appear in the right direction on the fabric once transferred. Each design printed on iron-on transfer paper should transfer onto fabric multiple times before it fades. The longer you iron, the darker and thicker the lines will be and the fewer transfers you'll get out of each design. The ink may fade with washing, but this is not guaranteed, so be sure to embroider over all the lines.

Once you've scanned and printed the design, cut it from the transfer sheet and place it facedown on your fabric. Press the back firmly with a hot, dry iron for 5 to 10 seconds. You can slide the iron gently over the design if necessary, but make sure it doesn't move and transfer double lines. Raise a corner of the transfer paper to check that the design has transferred properly before lifting it off the fabric.

Other transfer techniques: A water-soluble pen is a simple way to transfer a design. Make a photocopy of the motif and tape it to a window, which will act as a light box. Tape your fabric over the design and trace with the water-soluble pen.

For fabrics that are too dark or thick to use the window/light box method, you can use water-soluble fabric stabilizer. Using carbon paper, trace the design onto the stabilizer. Adhere the stabilizer to the front of the fabric. After you have placed your fabric and stabilizer in the hoop, you will stitch through the fabric and stabilizer together and then remove the stabilizer according to the package instructions.

THREADS

Cotton embroidery threads are made up of six strands twisted into one piece of thread, which you can split up into strands as needed. Cut a piece of thread about 16 inches long and divide it into the number of strands you need at one end. Then slide a finger between the strands and down the length of the thread to separate them.

Certain stitches turn out better when the individual strands have been split apart and regrouped before use. These include back, granitos, satin, and straight stitch. For stitches such as stem, chain, and others in which the individual strands aren't as visible, separating your thread into individual strands isn't always necessary.

When your stitches start looking thin and scraggly, your thread is likely stripped, or it has become too tightly twisted. If stripped, end off and start a new piece of thread. If too tightly wound, spin your needle between your thumb and forefinger to untwist it or turn your hoop upside down and let your needle dangle until the thread has untwisted itself.

The projects in this book use six-stranded, cotton DMC embroidery floss. DMC is one of the largest brands of embroidery floss and it is available at most craft and fabric stores. The colors listed in each pattern are labeled with a corresponding DMC color code number.

Stitching Guide

HOW TO START & END THREADS

To prevent your embroidery stitches from coming undone, you need to secure the start and end of each thread. Ways of doing this depend on personal preference and the stitch you intend to use. For example, use a knot when the lump it may make underneath the fabric won't be visible, like when embroidering French knots. Finish off each thread as you finish stitching to secure it, and cut off any excess so it won't get tangled in your working thread.

WASTE KNOT

For this temporary knot, knot the end of your thread on the front of the fabric, and then take the thread to the back of the fabric, about 3 or 4 inches away from where you're going to make your first stitch. Bring the thread to the front again to start embroidering. When done, cut the knot off and thread away on the back as you would to finish.

DOUBLE STITCH

If you're using backing fabric, only make a small double stitch through the backing fabric underneath the section you're about to embroider. Then bring the thread to the front and begin stitching. Cut off any excess thread.

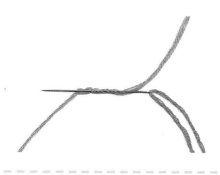

KNOT

Hold the tail end of your thread as well as the eye end of the needle between your thumb and forefinger and wrap the thread around the needle two or three times. Holding the thread taut in your other hand, pull the wraps of thread up the needle and under your thumb and forefinger, holding the eye end. Pull the needle through the loops to make a neat knot. Insert the needle directly below where you want to start to embroider.

FINISHING OFF

End off a row by taking your thread to the back of the fabric and securing it under the stitching. You are, in effect, whipping the back of the stitching (learn more about the whipped chain stitch on page 13). Secure it under a few stitches (at least five, more if necessary). You can also knot the thread, keeping it as close to the back of the fabric as possible, or make a small double stitch if you've used backing fabric.

STRAIGHT STITCH

The straight stitch is also known as an isolated satin stitch or stroke stitch. This simple stitch forms the basis of many other stitches, so it's covered first.

1. Come up at A and take your needle down again at B.

2. Pull the thread through until the stitch lies neatly on top of the fabric.

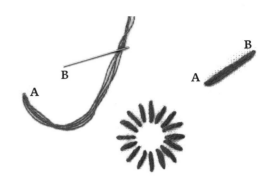

BACKSTITCH

The backstitch is good for lines and outlines, especially those with a lot of sharp points.

1. Bring the thread to the front of the fabric at A. Stick your needle into the fabric at B (the start of the line) and out again at C to create the first stitch. Continue in this way to the end of the row, using the same holes in the fabric at the start and end of each stitch.

2. To end the row, take your needle to the back of the fabric at D.

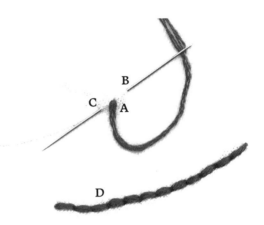

BACKSTITCH TRELLIS

To create a backstitch trellis, embroider intersecting rows of backstitch in a grid pattern in such a way that the stitches start and end at the intersections.

BLANKET STITCH

When the stitches are worked close together, blanket stitch is called buttonhole stitch. The solid line along the bottom edge of the stitches is known as the purl edge. This is a versatile stitch that was originally used to edge blankets and can be embroidered in a circle to create pinwheels.

1. Bring the thread up at A. Stick the needle into the fabric at B and reemerge at C, keeping the thread under the tip of the needle.

2. Take the needle to the back of the fabric at D to end a row, catching down the last blanket stitch.

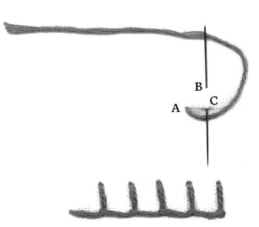

BLANKET STITCH PINWHEELS

Pinwheels can be embroidered with open or closed centers. For an open pinwheel, bring your thread up on the outer circle and insert your needle from inner to outer circle each time. Keep your needle perpendicular to the lines for a neat look. For a closed pinwheel, insert your needle through the same hole in the center of the circle each time. To finish, work your last blanket stitch so it just meets the start of your first, and then secure your thread with a straight stitch over the lower loop of the first blanket stitch.

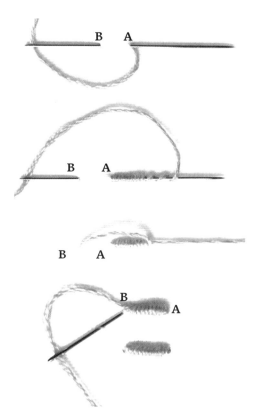

BULLION KNOT

Use a milliner/straw needle to create bullion knots. Although bullion knots can be tricky at first, once you get the hang of them, you'll find these versatile knots can be used as isolated stitches or packed together to fill an area with textured stitching.

1. Bring your thread to the front of the fabric at A. Take your needle to the back at B and reemerge at A. (Take care not to split the thread.)

2. Hold the eye of the needle against the fabric with your left thumb and use your right hand to wrap the thread around the tip of the needle until the length of wound thread measures the same as the distance between A and B. Keep the wraps even but not too tight around the needle. Holding the wraps of the knot between your thumb and forefinger, pull the needle through, drawing the thread through the wraps. (If you struggle with this step, rotate your needle in the opposite direction of the wraps to loosen them or try a bigger needle.)

3. Keep pulling the thread through the wraps until the top of the knot folds back toward B. If necessary, run your needle under the wraps while pulling on the thread to even them out. Take your thread to the back of the fabric at B to secure the knot.

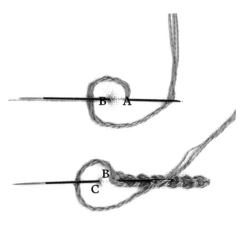

CHAIN STITCH

Chain stitch can be used for outlines, as well as in rows to fill or partially fill a shape. And it can be whipped in a similar or contrasting color thread to create a new stitch.

1. Bring the thread up at A and then take your needle back down through A and reemerge at B, keeping the thread under the tip of the needle. Pull the thread through until the first chain stitch is neatly looped around the emerging thread. Be careful not to pull too tightly or the stitch will distort. For the second and consecutive chain stitches, take the needle back in at B and reemerge at C.

2. To end off a row, make a small securing stitch by taking the thread down at D. To end off a closed shape such as a circle, come up at C and then slide your needle under the top of the first chain to create a mock chain stitch before taking your thread back down through C.

DETACHED CHAIN STITCH

Detached chain stitches are simply isolated chain stitches. They can be stitched along a line or arranged in rows to fill an area of a design. They make excellent flower petals and leaves.

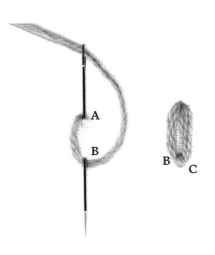

1. Bring the thread up at A, and then take your needle back down through A and reemerge at B, keeping the thread under the tip of the needle. Pull the thread through until the chain stitch is neatly looped around the emerging thread. Be careful not to pull too tightly or the stitch will distort.

2. Take the thread back down at C to complete the detached chain stitch.

LAZY DAISY STITCH

Detached chain stitches arranged in a flower shape are known as lazy daisy stitches. You can keep them separate and fill the center with one or more French knots, or come up through the same hole in the center each time.

TWISTED CHAIN STITCH

Twisted chain stitch is a beautifully textured stitch and can be used to embroider a single row or to fill a shape. Keep the length of each individual stitch as consistent as possible to create a neat row of embroidery.

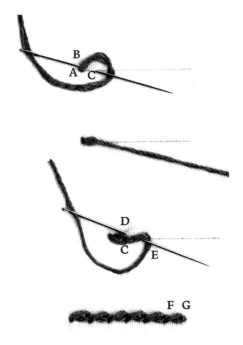

1. Bring your needle and thread up through the fabric at A. Insert your needle at B—a little to the left of A—and bring it up again on the line at C. Loop your thread around the tip of the needle. Pull the thread through to form the first twisted chain stitch.

2. Insert your needle at D, outside the first twisted chain stitch, and bring it up again on the line at E. Loop your thread around the needle tip and pull it through. Continue to the end of the row.

3. Finish with a small securing stitch over the lower edge of the last twisted chain stitch in the row, from F to G.

WHIPPED CHAIN STITCH

Bring your thread to the front at E. Slide the needle under the second chain stitch in the row, from right to left, without piercing the fabric. Whip the whole row or a section of the row of chain stitches in this way. To end off, take your thread to the back to the right of the last chain stitch.

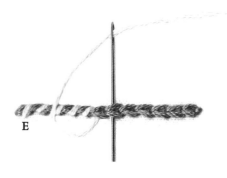

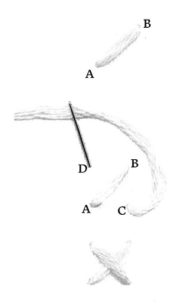

CROSS-STITCH

Cross-stitch is probably the most familiar embroidery stitch. It can be worked as an isolated stitch or in rows. The four points of each cross-stitch should form a square.

1. Bring your thread up at A and down at B to create the first half of the cross.

2. Bring the needle up at C and take it down again at D to complete the stitch.

3. Pull the thread through until the cross lies neatly on the fabric.

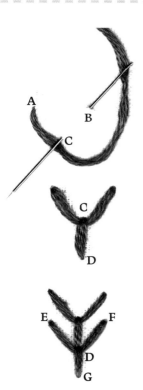

FLY STITCH

Fly stitches can be embroidered as standalone stitches or as a row of stitching. It is essentially an open detached chain stitch and is sometimes called a Y stitch because of its shape.

1. Bring your thread to the front at point A. Stick the needle into the fabric at B and reemerge at C, with the thread lying under the tip of the needle. Pull the thread through until the V of the fly stitch lies flush against the emerging thread.

2. Secure the stitch by taking your needle back down at D.

3. To stitch a row of fly stitches, bring your needle back up at E, and then take a stitch from F to D as you did for the first fly stitch. Take your thread back down at G to complete the second stitch. Continue this way to the end of the row.

FLY STITCH LEAF

Start with a straight stitch from the tip of the leaf down the central vein. Embroider a fly stitch below this, curving the V-shaped loop around the straight stitch and using a short securing stitch. Keep going as you would for a row of fly stitches, adjusting the angle and length of the V-shaped loop each time to fill the leaf shape.

FRENCH KNOT

Use a milliner/straw needle for knots. Traditionally, French knots were made by wrapping the thread around the needle just once, but today we tend to use more wraps.

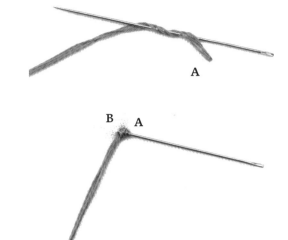

1. Bring your thread up at A. Hold your needle in one hand and wrap the thread over the needle twice with the other.

2. Hold the thread taut so the wraps don't slip off the end of the needle and twist it around to stick into your fabric at B—close to A, but not through the same hole. Pull the wraps of thread taut around the needle so that they lie against the fabric and keeping hold of your thread so the wraps don't come loose, pull your needle through to the back, drawing the thread through the loops to create the knot.

PISTIL STITCH

A pistil stitch is basically a French knot with a tail worked in the traditional way, with just one wrap of thread. Points A and B are farther apart, but the stitch is worked in the same way.

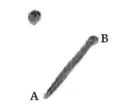

FOUR-LEGGED KNOT

This upright cross has a knot in the center. Four-legged knots can be worked as isolated stitches or scattered across an area of embroidery to fill it.

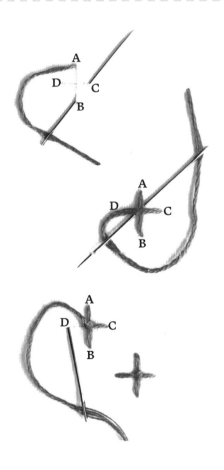

1. Bring your needle up at A, down at B, and up again at C to create the first upright stitch of the cross.

2. Lay your thread from C to D and hold it in place with your left thumb. Slide your needle under both threads in the center of the cross, from the upper right to the lower left, so your thread loops under the tip of the needle.

3. Pull the thread through gently to form the knot in the center of the cross, and take your needle down at D to finish the four-legged knot.

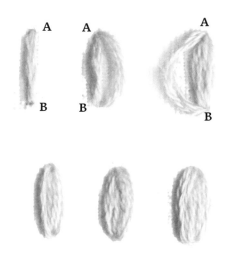

GRANITOS STITCH

Granitos, or "little grains," are made up of straight stitches worked through the same holes in the fabric to create plump, wheat-kernel shapes. They work well as smaller stitches, as they retain their shape better. You can use four or five stitches instead of three to create wider granitos.

1. Bring your thread to the front at A and make a straight stitch by taking it down again at B.

2. Bring your thread up again at A and down at B, positioning it so that the second stitch lies to the right of the first. Repeat so that your third stitch lies to the left of the first. If necessary, run your needle under the stitches so they puff up into granitos.

3. Use three, four, or five stitches for each granitos.

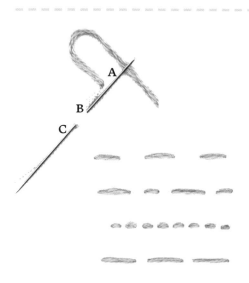

RUNNING STITCH

Running stitch is a simple stitch that can be spaced in various ways to different effect. Bear in mind when creating your own designs that sections of any line drawn onto your fabric will show, as running stitch doesn't cover the line completely.

1. Bring your thread up at A, and then take your needle down at B and reemerge at C.

2. Continue in this way to the end of the row, taking your thread to the back of the fabric to complete the last stitch.

3. Experiment with different lengths of stitches and gaps to create various effects with running stitch.

RHODES STITCH

Rhodes stitch is traditionally worked as a square on even-weave fabric. But when used to fill a circle in surface embroidery, it adds a three-dimensional element.

1. Bring your thread up at A and take it down again at B to create a vertical straight stitch across the center of the circle.

2. Bring your needle up again at C and take it down at D, so this stitch crosses over the first.

3. Keep working your way around the circle like this until it is filled with thread and the center is raised where each stitch crosses over the previous one. Make sure the stitches lie across the center of the circle each time and don't slide down the side of the "dome" as it gets higher.

SATIN STITCH

Satin stitch fills an area with straight stitches. To make it easier, do it as a stab stitch: bring your thread up through the fabric and take it down in two actions. Begin in the middle of the area you want to fill and stitch outward, then return to the center and fill the other half. The shape to be filled dictates the direction of your stitches. Follow any curves by increasing the space between stitches along one edge and decreasing on the other.

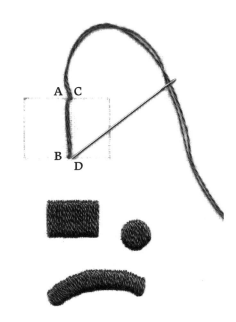

1. Bring your thread to the front of the fabric at A and take it down again at B as you would to make a straight stitch. Come up again at C and take your thread to the back again at D to create the next stitch.

2. Continue in this way until the entire area is filled with dense stitching.

PADDED SATIN STITCH

Padded satin stitch is made up of layers of satin stitching. Start with a layer that doesn't quite reach the outlines of the final shape. Then embroider another layer of satin stitch over this, filling the shape. You can use two, three, or more layers to give added height. Embroider each layer perpendicular to the last.

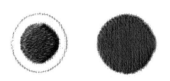

STAR STITCH

Star stitch is an isolated stitch that can be scattered randomly over an area or worked in a grid pattern for a more uniform look.

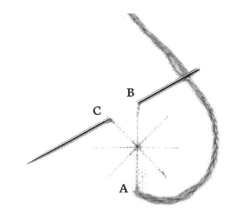

1. Come up at A. Stick your needle into the fabric at B and reemerge at C. Pull your thread through to make the first stitch.

2. Do the same from D to E and F to G, and then take your thread to the back at H.

3. Complete the star stitch by catching it down with a small stitch from I to J.

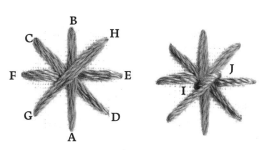

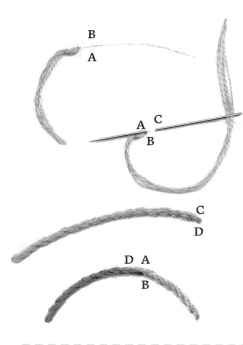

STEM STITCH

Stem stitch is good for outlines. The tricks are to bring your needle up through the hole at the end of the prior stitch and to always keep your thread below your needle.

1. Bring your thread up at A and, working from left to right, make the first stitch from B to A. Your thread should reemerge through the same hole at A.

2. Keep your thread below your needle at all times, and make the next stitch from C to B, bringing your needle up through the same hole at B. Continue stitching along the line in this way.

3. To end off a row of stem stitch, make the last stitch from D to C, and then take the needle back down at D. For a closed shape such as a circle, make the last stitch from A to D, and then take your needle back down again at B (covering your first small stitch) to hide the join.

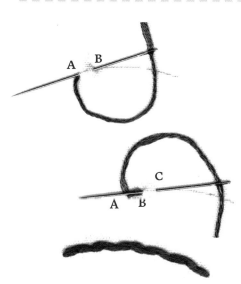

CABLE STEM STITCH

Cable stem stitch is done in a similar manner to stem stitch. It is sometimes called cable outline stitch or alternating stem stitch.

1. Working from left to right, bring your needle and thread up through the fabric at A and take your first stitch from B to A, with the thread below the needle. Your needle should reemerge at A.

2. Take your next stitch from C to B, but this time make sure your thread is lying above your needle.

3. Position your thread below your needle again for the next stitch and continue along the row in this way, with your thread alternating below and above the needle for each stitch. Take your thread down through the same hole in the fabric as your last stitch to finish the row.

WOVEN SPIDER WEB STITCH

Woven spider web stitch , or woven stitch, creates a raised circle of textured stitching.

1. Embroider seven straight stitches radiating from the center of the circle. Take your thread down through the same hole at the center each time. Bring your thread up under one of these stitches, as close to the center as possible, and begin weaving over and under the straight stitches.

2. Continue weaving over and under the foundation stitches in an outward spiral, taking care not to pierce the fabric, until the circle is filled with thread. If you went under a foundation stitch on the previous round, go over it the next time.

3. Finish by taking your thread down under a foundation stitch, as if you're going to weave under it.

More Stitches

WEAVE STITCH

Stitch a horizontal satin stitch, but instead of placing the rows close together, leave a little bit of space between them. Now you can do the vertical stitches. Start in the right-top corner by stitching from the back to the front. Then weave your needle through the horizontal stitches by pulling it over and under the stitches until you reach the top-left corner. When you come to the end, stitch to the back and start the next row. Continue this pattern until you've finished the whole space.

WHIPPED BACKSTITCH

The whipped backstitch is just an upgrade to the normal backstitch. After making a backstitch, go back to the start, and stitch from the back to the front, close to the first stitch you made. Then pull your needle and floss under every stitch. Always do this from the same side to create a whipped look, like a candy cane.

JENNY BILLINGHAM

Rainbow

An embroidered rainbow is a great project for using up leftover threads from previous projects. I've chosen colors that include pinks, oranges, yellows, greens, blues, and purples, but you could use any combination of colors you like. See below for some color thread suggestions, and remember that you can change it up however you want.

TOOLS & MATERIALS

- » Fabric: cotton, cotton twill, and/or cotton linen blend
- » Embroidery needles
- » 6- or 7-inch embroidery hoop
- » Embroidery and fabric scissors
- » Erasable pen
- » 100% cotton yarn, DK (double-knit) weight in a shade of white
- » Cotton thread for securing the fabric on the back (optional)
- » Felt

THREAD COLORS

Purples:
- DMC 29 Eggplant
- DMC 30 Medium Light Blueberry
- DMC 210 Medium Lavender
- DMC 3743 Very Light Antique Violet

Blues:
- DMC 334 Medium Baby Blue
- DMC 800 Pale Delft Blue
- DMC 809 Delft Blue
- DMC 3839 Medium Lavender Blue

Greens:
- DMC 368 Light Pistachio Green
- DMC 564 Very Light Jade
- DMC 703 Chartreuse
- DMC 772 Very Light Yellow Green

Yellows:
- DMC 728 Topaz
- DMC 745 Light Pale Yellow
- DMC 973 Bright Canary
- DMC 3822 Light Straw

Oranges:
- DMC 721 Medium Orange Spice
- DMC 754 Light Peach
- DMC 967 Very Light Apricot
- DMC 3341 Apricot

Pinks:
- DMC 778 Very Light Antique Mauve
- DMC 956 Geranium
- DMC 961 Dark Dusty Rose
- DMC 3726 Dark Antique Mauve

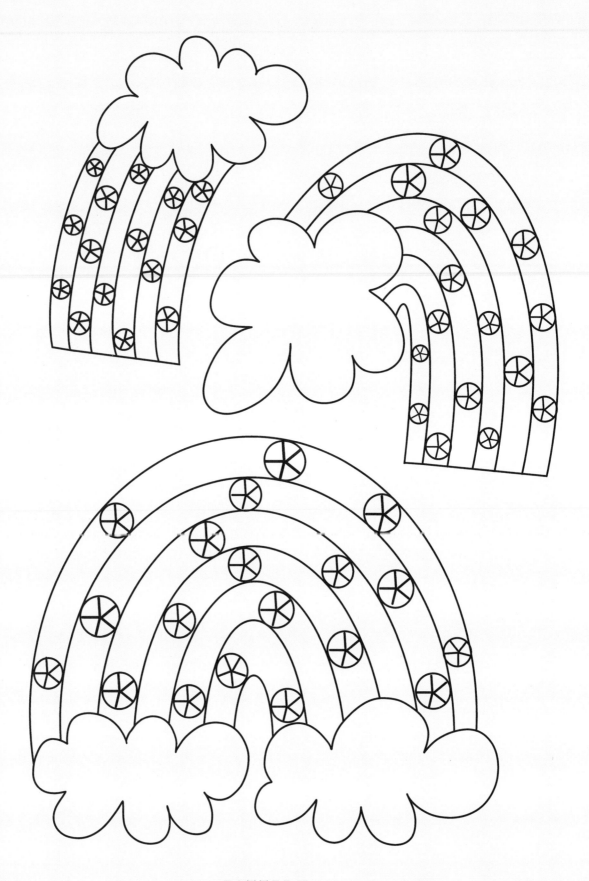

PATTERN

Note: This pattern is to scale for a 6-inch hoop.

Step 1

Choose a rainbow from the selection of designs (page 22) and frame your fabric in the embroidery hoop. For thinner fabrics, you can double up the layers to create more tension and a taut, flat surface to stitch on. Using an erasable pen, trace the outline of the design onto the fabric you've prepared for stitching.

For help with tracing the design, frame the fabric in reverse so that it can be laid flat on a hard surface, light box, or window. (See image). Once traced, reframe it before stitching.

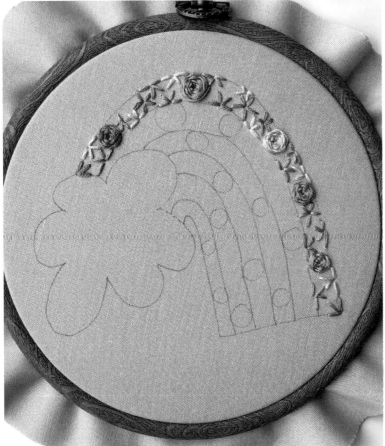

Step 2

Start the embroidery design by stitching woven wheels in the first line of the rainbow. Use all six strands of thread for each stitch. Then add straight stitches to create star shapes in random places and colors along the same line. Using a variety of tones for each section really adds to the effect of a rainbow.

Step 3

Fill the remainder of the line with a dense bed of French knots. Make sure to stitch these really close together for lots of texture and no gaps.

Step 4

Repeat steps 2 and 3 as you work through the rainbow colors, starting always with the largest woven wheels, then the straight stitches, and then the French knots to fill in all the gaps.

Step 5

For the cloud, use a darning needle and 100% cotton yarn to stitch fluffy French knots. As before, keep them very close together.

For extra-chunky French knots, wrap the thread around the needle five times. This gives a three-dimensional texture that works beautifully for clouds.

Step 6

Once the design is complete, trim any excess fabric away, leaving approximately ⅓ inch around the edge of the hoop. Sew a running stitch around the fabric and gather neatly at the back, securing tightly. This can be left as is or covered with felt.

Buying Locally & Supporting Independent Shops

SHOPPING LOCALLY is one of my passions; if I can find a small independent shop to buy my craft supplies from, I will always opt for it over larger stores. On day trips and holidays, I get excited to find new places I've not visited before. Small shops are like Aladdin's caves, with wonderful selections of fabrics, yarns, threads, and embellishments. I find being able to touch fabrics really makes a difference. My embroidery work is often very dense and detailed, and I like to use fabrics that have the least amount of stretch in them. Heavier cottons and twills are perfect and some of my favorites. Independent shops offer so much inspiration, and quite often they have little offcuts of fabric you can purchase that are the perfect size for embroidery hoops.

I also love finding vintage and secondhand shops. These are always full of unusual things: old sewing boxes, craft storage, vintage fabrics, and fashion pieces, just to mention a few! I once found an old jewelry stand that I now use to hang little embroidery hoops from.

Denim is my favorite type of clothing to embroider, and in the vintage shops, you'll find so many gorgeous denim items. These are quite often branded and superb quality.

I have discovered so many unique fabric pieces in vintage shops. Lace can be found very easily, and using vintage lace gives a lovely effect. It is beautiful when layered over colored fabric to create texture, and you can add your embroidery over the top.

Visiting independent shops not only offers unique finds, but it also gives you a chance to build a relationship with the shop owners too. They can be a second pair of eyes. I have found that they will look out for things they think you will like and let you know about them. I love shopping small.

FAQs

How long does embroidery take?

Embroidery takes as long as you would like it too! This is why I love embroidery. Some days I can stitch for hours, while other days I just stitch a tiny section of my design. The best thing about embroidery is that it can be put away and brought out again so easily. There are so many hoop sizes out there. You can start off small, and as confidence grows, so can your designs.

When did you start doing embroidery?

I started doing embroidery in January 2020. I found an old box full of embroidery threads while clearing out my craft room storage. I used to use them for making friendship bracelets when I was a child. I had an embroidery hoop from when I'd once tried cross-stitch. The first design I stitched was a trio of cacti in pretty pots.

How did you learn?

I learned by watching YouTube videos and from embroidery books I had borrowed from the library.

Where do you find your inspiration?

It's all around me all the time, especially in wildflower gardens. I love walking through them, taking photos on my phone. My daughters have also inspired a lot of my designs. Their love for rainbows and stars has enabled me to create many designs using simple shapes and outlines.

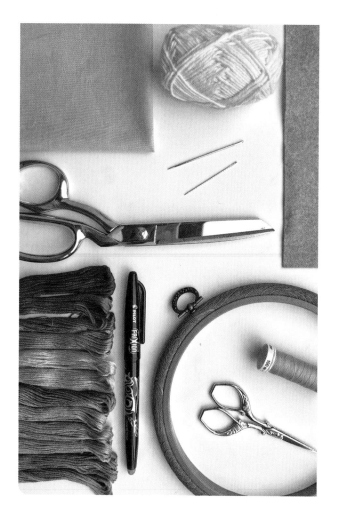

How do you wash embroidered clothing?

Embroidered clothing can be machine washed, but washing guidelines need to be adhered to. Good-quality threads are essential, and their own instructions should be followed.

What are the best needles to use?

I have a wide range of needles that I like to use. These include standard embroidery needles but also darning, quilting, ballpoint, and more.

How do you back your hoops?

I back most of my hoops with felt, gathering the edges of the fabric at the back first. I then blanket stitch a circle of felt over the top to cover the back of the embroidery.

Which pen do you use to draw your designs?

I use Pilot® FriXion® pens for my designs; they are erasable and come in a huge range of colors. You can also get highlighters, gel, and roller balls in the range.

Which hoops do you prefer to use?

I love using the woodgrain flexible hoops. They are very simple to use and are also great for displaying the finished embroidery.

How do you store your threads?

I have several ways of storing my threads. Some ways are quirkier than others! I first stored my threads on twigs and branches I found on a spring walk—I popped them in a jar and hung the threads off the ends. It looked great. I also use the card bobbins and sometimes pegs. Another great way to store them is using a peg board with hooks.

What fabric do you use?

My favorite fabrics to use are cotton twills and cotton-linen blends. I prefer heavier fabrics with little stretch.

What are the best threads?

My personal favorites are DMC or Anchor. The colors are washable and fade-resistant. I find the colors are reliable and consistent, and they both work beautifully on clothes.

How many strands do you use?

It definitely varies by design, but I tend to use two, three, and six. I definitely prefer to use six strands for French knots and woven wheels.

Creating Your Own Patterns

CREATING PATTERNS is one of my favorite processes. I love taking photographs when I go out for walks, and these are often a fantastic source for my embroidery designs. I'm always taking photos just in case!

If you're already an artsy person who likes to doodle and draw, designing an embroidery pattern can be as easy as sketching an image on plain paper and then transferring the design to the fabric using a light box or window. You can even draw your motifs straight onto the fabric. If you're brave enough to try this method, I would highly recommend Pilot FriXion pens. They are removable with heat. I like to use my hair dryer for this, but it is always best to test the pens on excess fabric first. Knowing there is the freedom to erase a section of the design, if it doesn't go quite to plan, is very reassuring! Drawing directly onto the fabric may sound scary at first, but it's something you will get more confident doing over time.

To design my patterns on paper, I like to draw around the center ring of the embroidery hoop. This gives the initial template and size guide. You should always consider the stitches you'd like to use, those you know or feel comfortable with or perhaps the ones you'd like to learn. The size of the hoop is really important. When I began my embroidery journey, I found large hoops very scary and daunting! I always opted for the smallest size, a 3-inch hoop, for example. Stitching in smaller hoops first allows you to complete a design more quickly and confidently.

Another of my go-to pattern tools are cookie cutters! It's a personal favorite! It may sound a bit strange, but these are amazing outlines for embroidery designs. There are so many shapes out there. You can use these as a simple outline and draw in the remaining elements.

If you're less confident with your drawing skills, tracing is great and very quick. Try tracing from your own photos or perhaps your favorite books. It's a lovely way to find beautiful images of flowers and wildlife that can be put together to make a gorgeous template.

Embroidery can also be very abstract and random and all about the texture. By choosing a bold-colored background fabric, you can use up all those threads and yarns that you have left over. Simply use the stitches you love the most to build up a design in an organic way. Layering up or stitching in block colors can be effective. You can also think about adding 3D elements, such as beads, ribbons, or buttons. Decorative stitches in bold colors can be just as exciting as an image.

If you feel more at ease with designing patterns, Procreate is the perfect tool for more detailed and precise designs. You can trace over your own photos, add lettering, and be really experimental with color palettes.

JENNY BILLINGHAM

Denim Pocket Garden

If you don't have a denim jacket to embroider on, see page 26 for advice on where to source used and locally sold denim and other fabric pieces for your projects.

TOOLS & MATERIALS	THREAD COLOR GUIDE
» Denim jacket or jeans	● DMC 370 Medium Mustard
» Embroidery needles	● DMC 407 Dark Desert Sand
» 6- or 7-inch embroidery hoop	○ DMC 415 Pearl Gray
» Embroidery and fabric scissors	● DMC 452 Medium Shell Gray
» Erasable pen	● DMC 647 Medium Beaver Gray
» Sticky soluble stabilizer	○ DMC 712 Cream
» Stranded cotton embroidery thread (see color guide, or stitch in your own choice of colors)	○ DMC 928 Very Light Gray Green
» Sulky® Tender Touch Cover-a-Stitch stabilizer	● DMC 3771 Ultra Very Light Terra Cotta
	○ DMC 3779 Very Light Rosewood
	● DMC 3813 Light Blue Green
	● DMC 3859 Light Rosewood

PATTERN

Note: This pattern is to scale for a 6-inch hoop.

Step 1

To begin, trace the floral design onto the sticky soluble stabilizer using an erasable pen and position it over the pocket. Frame the design with the embroidery hoop, and you're ready to stitch.

Step 2

Starting with the flower on the far left, satin stitch the petals in three strands of terracotta (DMC 3859). Next, stitch the other flower petals in the following sequence: salmon pink (DMC 3779), mushroom (DMC 452), cream (DMC 712), fawn (DMC 407), and peach (DMC 3771).

Step 3

For the flower centers, use six strands and sew French knots. Start with the far-left flower and use seafoam (DMC 928) then powder blue (DMC 415), and follow with mint (DMC 3813). Repeat for the other three flowers.

Step 4

Backstitch the stems of the flowers in three strands of olive (DMC 370), and then satin stitch the leaves. For the grass, use three strands of sage (DMC 647) and straight stitch the blades of grass.

Use the template as a guide for the grass. To give a sense of depth, take some stitches over the flowers and stems.

Step 5

For symmetry, repeat the design in reverse on the second pocket if you wish. When all the stitching is complete, submerge the embroidered area in warm water and agitate the design to remove the soluble stabilizer. This will take a few minutes, but it will all dissolve.

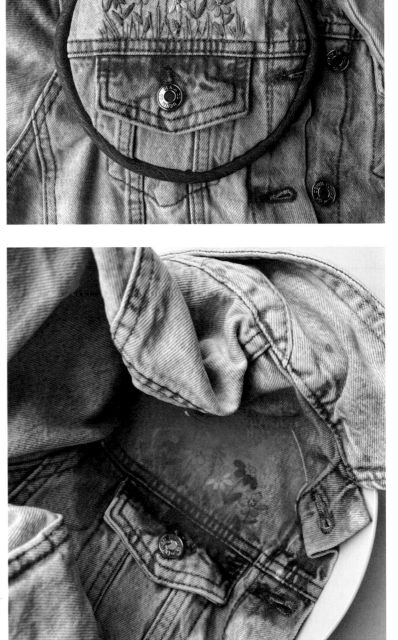

Step 6

Trim and secure the stitches tightly at the back. Then iron on the Cover-a-Stitch to protect the design on the reverse. This fabric's smooth texture also prevents irritation to the skin.

Warm water removes the soluble stabilizer more effectively than cold.

JENNY BILLINGHAM

Shooting Stars

This piece featuring shooting stars would make a lovely baby gift for hanging in a nursery.

TOOLS & MATERIALS	THREAD COLOR GUIDE
» Fabric: cotton twill, cotton, Kona cotton	● DMC 21 Light Alizarin
» Embroidery needles	● DMC 518 Light Wedgwood
» 7-inch embroidery hoop	● DMC 562 Medium Jade
» Embroidery and fabric scissors	● DMC 676 Light Old Gold
» Erasable pen	● DMC 832 Golden Olive
» Metallic gold fabric marker	● DMC 3350 Ultra Dark Dusty Rose
» Stranded cotton embroidery thread	● DMC 3835 Medium Grape
» Cotton thread (optional)	
» Felt	

PATTERN

Note: This pattern is to scale for a 7-inch hoop.

Step 1

Trace the shooting star design onto your fabric with erasable pen and frame in the hoop so you're ready for stitching.

Step 2

Using the fabric marker, color in the center areas of the stars. Depending on the fabric you chose, it may take a couple of layers to cover.

Step 3

Next, satin stitch the outline of the stars in three strands of gold (DMC 832), creating a border around the fabric-painted areas.

To make the design more unique, why not add some of your own patterns to the center of the stars over the top of the gold fabric marker? Use your erasable pen to draw out your pattern and stitch the design in the same gold thread.

Step 4

Chain stitch the lines coming from the stars. Use six strands for each color: pink (DMC 3350), orange (DMC 21), yellow (DMC 676), green (DMC 562), blue (DMC 518), and purple (DMC 3835).

Future Project Idea!

You could also embroider this design on a sweatshirt or T-shirt. Trace the design on a sticky soluble stabilizer and stitch the motif onto the garment. The center of the stars could be left open with the fabric showing through, or you could fill the middle with some beautiful French knots.

Step 5

When the stitching is complete, trim the excess fabric around the hoop, leaving a ⅓-inch overhang. Sew a running stitch around the fabric and gather it tightly at the back. To protect the design, sew a circle of felt to the reverse.

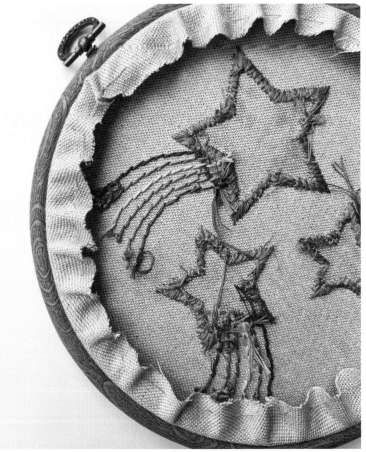

JENNY BILLINGHAM

Embellished Sweatshirt

Sweatshirts with a higher cotton percentage are easier to stitch than those with stretch. If your sweatshirt does stretch, a fusible interfacing on the reverse will help the tension of the fabric when framed in the hoop, making stitching easier. Comfy, cozy sweatshirts make perfect embroidery garments. They come in so many colors and are quite often made from organic or recycled fibers.

TOOLS & MATERIALS	THREAD COLOR GUIDE
» Sweatshirt	● DMC 223 Light Shell Pink
» Embroidery needles	● DMC 315 Medium Dark Antique Mauve
» 8-inch embroidery hoop	● DMC 316 Medium Antique Mauve
» Embroidery and fabric scissors	○ DMC 543 Ultra Very Light Beige
» Erasable pen	● DMC 676 Light Old Gold
» Sticky soluble stabilizer	○ DMC 677 Very Light Old Gold
» Stranded cotton embroidery thread	● DMC 778 Very Light Antique Mauve
» Sulky Tender Touch Cover-a-Stitch stabilizer	● DMC 977 Light Golden Brown
	● DMC 3011 Dark Khaki Green
	● DMC 3022 Medium Brown Gray
	● DMC 3052 Medium Green Gray
	● DMC 3350 Ultra Dark Dusty Rose
	● DMC 3687 Mauve
	● DMC 3776 Light Mahogany
	● DMC 3778 Light Terra Cotta
	● DMC 3813 Light Blue Green
	● DMC 3817 Light Celadon Green

PATTERN

Note: This pattern is to scale for an 8-inch hoop.

Step 1

Trace the floral design onto the sticky soluble stabilizer using an erasable pen. Position the pattern on the left shoulder and stick it to the sweatshirt fabric. Frame the design with the 8-inch embroidery hoop, and you're ready to stitch.

Step 2

For the large pink flower, satin stitch the petals in three strands of deep pink (DMC 3350). Next, stitch the small pale pink flecks on the lower parts of the petals using six strands of blush (DMC 778). For the flower center, use six strands of tangerine (DMC 977) and satin stitch the middle circle. For the large yellow flower, satin stitch the petals in three strands of honey (DMC 676). Add three straight stitches to each petal in six strands of lemon (DMC 677). Finally, stitch French knots in the flower center using six strands of pink (DMC 316).

Step 3

Satin stitch the orange flower petals in three strands of orange (DMC 3776), and use rose (DMC 3687) to add a single straight stitch to the base of the petals. In the center, stitch one French knot in six strands of beige (DMC 543). Next, use three strands of mulberry (DMC 315) and satin stitch the second flower's petals. Fill the center with French knots in six strands of blush (DMC 778).

Step 4

Satin stitch the petals of the four daisies in three strands of beige (DMC 543). In the centers, stitch one French knot in six strands of coral (DMC 3778). In the largest daisy, stitch three French knots. For the pink blooms, single chain stitch the petals in six strands of rose (DMC 3687). Over the top, stitch three more single chain stitches in aqua (DMC 3813). These overlap the pink. Backstitch the stems in the same color.

Step 5

Satin stitch the yellow daisy in six strands of lemon (DMC 677), and then satin stitch the center in six strands of duck egg (DMC 3817). Backstitch the stems of the berry branch in six strands of sage (DMC 3022). For the berries, sew three French knots at the end of each stem using six strands of dusky pink (DMC 223).

Step 6

Fishbone stitch the leaves of the large branch in six strands of moss (DMC 3052). Then backstitch the stem. For the green, chain stitch branches using six strands of olive (DMC 3011). Stitch the leaves first and then the stem. Finally, stitch the last chain stitch branches in three stands of mulberry (DMC 315). In the center of the chain stitches, add one straight stitch to fill the space.

Step 7

When the stitching is complete, submerge the fabric to soak off the soluble stabilizer. Cover the stitches on the reverse using the Cover-a-Stitch backing to protect the design and prevent rubbing on the skin.

JENNY BILLINGHAM

Houseplant

If you are anything like me, you love a houseplant...or two or three. Often the real ones don't last long, but this design will be around forever! When stitching the leaves, make sure you follow the direction of the leaf to create a more realistic effect.

TOOLS & MATERIALS	THREAD COLOR GUIDE
» Fabric: cotton, cotton twill, cotton-linen blend	● DMC 161 Gray Blue
» Embroidery needles	● DMC 370 Medium Mustard
» 6-inch embroidery hoop	● DMC 934 Black Avocado Green
» Embroidery and fabric scissors	● DMC 3011 Dark Khaki Green
» Erasable pen	● DMC 3687 Mauve
» Stranded cotton embroidery thread	● DMC 3778 Light Terra Cotta
	● DMC 3817 Light Celadon Green
» Felt	● DMC 3822 Light Straw

PATTERN

Note: This pattern is to scale for a 6-inch hoop.

Step 1

Trace the houseplant design onto the fabric and frame it with the embroidery hoop.

Step 2

The leaves are created with a combination of three different green thread colors. To do this, you need to take a single strand of each green—pine (DMC 934), pickle (DMC 3011), and fern (DMC 370)—and thread them all through the needle together. This will give a beautiful tonal effect. Each leaf is then stitched using a fishbone stitch.

Step 3

For the stems, use pine (DMC 934) and backstitch in three strands.

Step 4

Brick stitch the main section of the plant pot in six strands of gray blue (DMC 161).

Step 5

For the zigzags, satin stitch the lines in three strands of each color: pink (DMC 3687), light terra cotta (DMC 3778), lemon (DMC 3822), and aqua (DMC 3817).

Step 6

When the embroidery is complete, trim the excess fabric at the back. Gather the edges using a running stitch. Cut a circle in the felt and sew it on to cover the back.

JENNY BILLINGHAM

Trio of Hearts T-shirt

This design is very random, and the beauty of it is that you can customize the placement of your colors. I have chosen a rainbow palette, but you could use threads of the same tone or even one single color, depending on your T-shirt color and style.

TOOLS & MATERIALS	THREAD COLOR GUIDE
» T-shirt	● DMC 316 Medium Antique Mauve
» Embroidery needles	● DMC 368 Light Pistachio Green
» 8-inch embroidery hoop	● DMC 402 Very Light Mahogany
» Embroidery and fabric scissors	● DMC 580 Dark Moss Green
» Erasable pen	● DMC 597 Turquoise
» Sticky soluble stabilizer	● DMC 600 Very Dark Cranberry
» Stranded cotton embroidery thread	● DMC 743 Medium Yellow
» Sulky Tender Touch Cover-a-Stitch stabilizer	● DMC 793 Medium Cornflower Blue
	● DMC 3776 Light Mahogany
	● DMC 3822 Light Straw
	● DMC 3833 Light Raspberry
	● DMC 3835 Medium Grape

PATTERN

Note: This pattern is to scale for an 8-inch hoop.

Step 1

To begin, trace your choice of heart trio onto the soluble stabilizer. The design can be placed across the front of the garment or on the shoulder, or you could use a single heart on the chest. Once the design has been positioned, frame the design with your embroidery hoop, and you're ready for stitching.

For thinner or stretchy T-shirts, you can use a tear-away stabilizer on the reverse of the shirt.

Step 2

Start by stitching the lazy daisies first. These are the largest stitches on the garment, and once these are stitched, it is easier to distribute the other color threads throughout the design. Use six strands. Add a single French knot to the center of each daisy in a contrast color.

Step 3

Once all the lazy daisies are stitched, begin adding the star elements. These are made up of straight stitches, again using six strands.

Step 4

Next, fill in the gaps with French knots in six strands of thread. Use a mixture of colors and distribute them throughout all the hearts.

Try to trim your threads as much as you can at the back of the T-shirt rather than having long threads hanging between each design to avoid catching them when embroidering.

Step 5

When the embroidery is finished, submerge the garment in water to remove the stabilizer. This may take a few minutes.

Step 6

When the T-shirt has dried, trim any loose threads and apply the Cover-a-Stitch to the reverse of the embroidery. This will add a layer of protection for both your stitching and skin.

THERESA WENSING

Flower Meadow

When you look at this cute design, it almost feels like you can smell the flower meadow. This design is perfect for spreading summer vibes in your home, but it's also perfect for practicing basic stitches like stem stitch, satin stitch, and French knot stitch.

TOOLS & MATERIALS	THREAD COLOR GUIDE
» Stranded cotton embroidery thread	● DMC 159 Light Gray Blue
» Embroidery needles	● DMC 167 Very Dark Yellow Beige
» 6-inch embroidery hoop	● DMC 924 Very Dark Gray Green
» White cotton fabric	● DMC 926 Medium Gray Green
» Embroidery and fabric scissors	● DMC 945 Tawny
	● DMC 3012 Medium Khaki Green
	● DMC 3771 Ultra Very Light Terra Cotta
	○ DMC 3866 Ultra Very Light Mocha

PATTERN

Note: This pattern is to scale for a 6-inch hoop.

Step 1

Prepare your hoop
(see page 7).

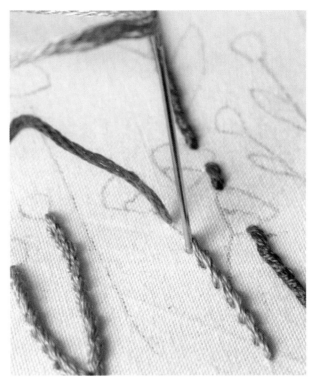

Step 2

Start by stitching all the dark green stems with whipped backstitch and DMC 924 (very dark gray green). Use six strands.

Step 3

Stitch the lighter green stems with DMC 926 (medium gray green) and stem stitch. Use six strands.

Step 4

For the khaki-colored stems, use six strands and split stitch with DMC 3012 (medium khaki green).

Step 5

For the hay, stitch a reverse chain stitch with six strands. Use DMC 167 (very dark yellow beige).

Step 6

Use six strands and satin stitch for all the leaves. Match the leaf colors to the stems.

Step 7

For the beige and pink blossoms, repeat step 6. Use DMC 3771 (ultra very light terra cotta) and 945 (tawny).

Step 8

For the remaining blossoms, use a French knot stitch with six strands. Use DMC 159 (light gray blue) for the lavender blossoms and DMC 3866 (ultra very light mocha) for the little dots. Do two turns for DMC 159. For DMC 3866, do one turn for the little knots and three turns for the big knots.

Finish the Hoop

To finish the hoop, cut the fabric into a circle, leaving a little space around the frame. Pull the fabric tight. Grab a few inches of thread and do a simple running stitch around the whole hoop, leaving a small space between the thread and the frame. When you are back to where you started, pull the ends and see how the fabric wraps around the hoop. Knot the ends and you're done!

Step 9

Finish the hoop, and remove any visible lines from the transfer pen.

THERESA WENSING

Daisies

Would you love to spread a springlike atmosphere all year round? Then this hoop is the right project for you. The cute little daisies will enrich every room with a spring feeling—you can almost smell them!

TOOLS & MATERIALS	THREAD COLOR GUIDE
» Stranded cotton embroidery thread	○ DMC 01 White Tin
» Embroidery needles	● DMC 3827 Pale Golden Brown
» 6-inch embroidery hoop	
» Beige linen fabric	
» Embroidery and fabric scissors	

PATTERN

Note: This pattern is to scale for a 6-inch hoop.

Step 1

Transfer your design onto the fabric of your choice and place it in a 6-inch hoop.

Step 2

Start stitching the blossoms with a satin stitch and DMC 01. Use the full six strands for a chunky look. To create a more delicate look, use only three strands. Work from the outside in as you create your stitches.

Repeat with each of the ten flowers.

Step 3

Now fill the centers of the flowers with French knots and DMC 3827. Use six strands and two turns. When you want a smaller, more delicate look, do just one turn or use three strands instead of six.

Start in the middle of each blossom and first embroider to the one side, and then embroider to the other side. This makes it easier to get a nice curve on the outside of the blossom.

Step 4

Repeat step 3 with each of the 10 flowers. It doesn't matter if you go in a circle or fill it from right to left. The main thing is to make enough knots so that you don't see any fabric through them.

Step 5

Now you're ready to finish your hoop. Remove the still-visible lines using the instructions on your transfer pen.

Step 6

Finish your hoop by attaching fabric to it (see page 65 for instructions).

THERESA WENSING

Cup of Planets

Instead of having a cup of tea, have a cup of planets. This design pays homage not just to the beautiful world but the whole universe. Appreciate it by creating this!

TOOLS & MATERIALS	THREAD COLOR GUIDE
» Stranded cotton embroidery thread	○ DMC 01 White Tin
» Embroidery needles	● DMC 310 Black
» 9-inch embroidery hoop	◐ DMC 316 Medium Antique Mauve
» White cotton fabric	◑ DMC 341 Light Blue Violet
» Embroidery and fabric scissors	◓ DMC 729 Medium Old Gold
	○ DMC 761 Light Salmon
	○ DMC 775 Very Light Baby Blue
	○ DMC 3823 Ultra Pale Yellow

PATTERN

Note: This pattern is to scale for a 9-inch hoop.

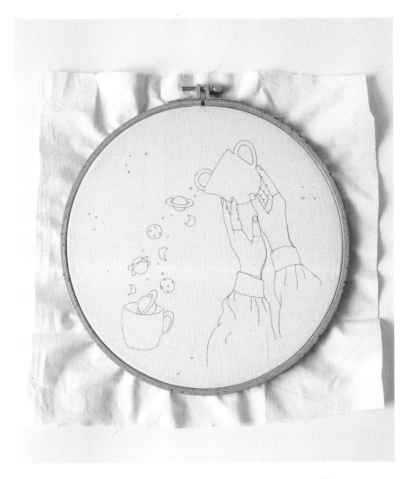

Step 1

Transfer your design to the fabric and place it into a 9-inch hoop.

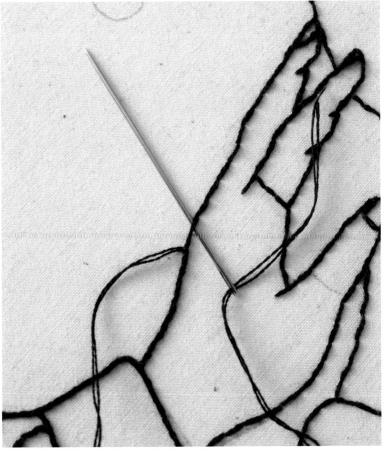

Step 2

Start stitching the hands and the cups using DMC 310 (black) with two strands and whipped backstitch.

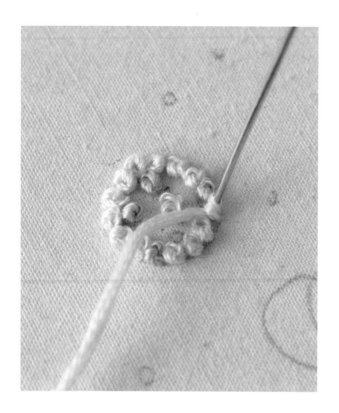

Step 3

Stitch the light blue planets with DMC 775 (light baby blue) and 761 (light salmon). Use six strands and French knots with one turn. Start with the pink knots, and then do the outline and fill with blue knots.

Step 4

For the two rings of this planet, use two strands and whipped backstitch. Use DMC 01 (white).

Step 5

After you complete the rings, fill in the planet with satin stitch. Stitch from right to left using DMC 316 (mauve) and six strands.

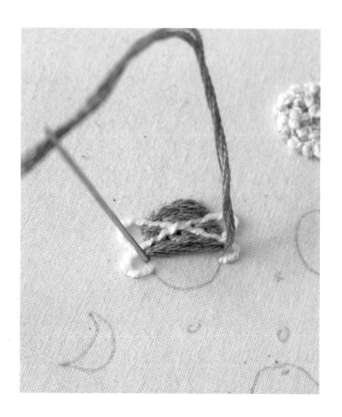

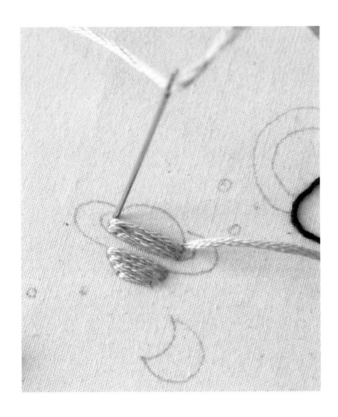

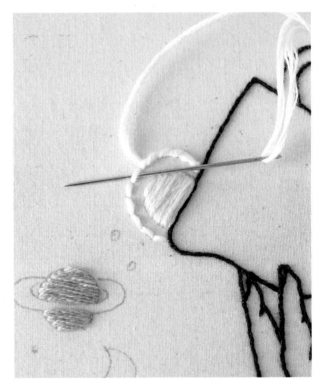

Step 6

Fill in the rest of the planets with six strands and satin stitch using DMC 341 (light blue violet) and DMC 775 (light baby blue).

Step 7

To create the white ring around this planet, do a whipped backstitch with six strands. Use DMC 01 (white).

Step 8

For the yellow rings around the purple planets, do a reverse chain stitch with six strands of DMC 3823.

Step 9

For the moons, start stitching the outside with split stitch and six strands using DMC 729 (medium old gold). Then fill in the inside. Repeat for all three moons.

Step 10

Do the small dots with French knot stitch and six strands using DMC 3823 (pale yellow). To create smaller and bigger dots, you can change the number of turns. Do one turn for a small dot and two or three turns for a bigger dot.

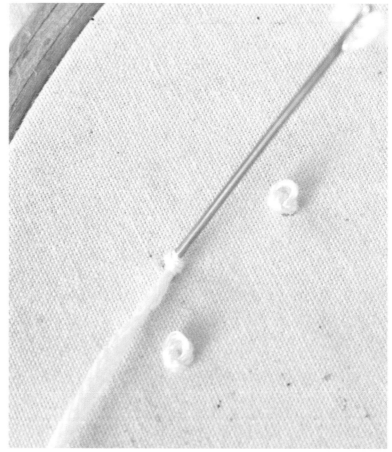

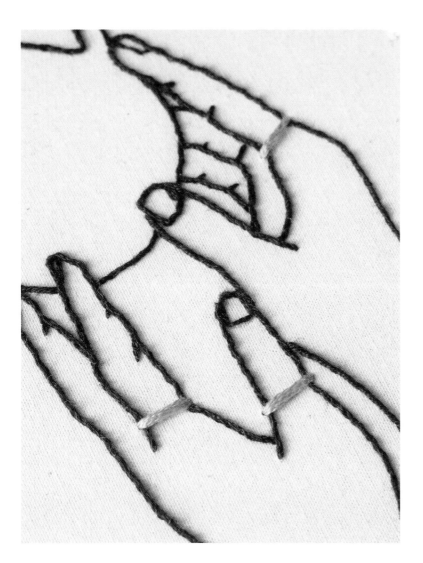

Step 11

Stitch the rings with DMC 729 (medium old gold), just one simple stitch from one side to the other. Repeat that with all three rings.

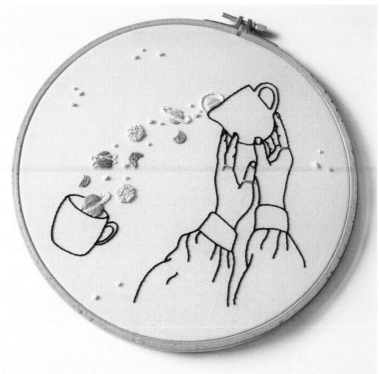

Step 12

Remove visible transfer pen lines, following the instructions on your transfer pen, and finish your hoop.

THERESA WENSING

Cute Camper

This project is for all those people with wanderlust. Transport yourself by stitching this cute little caravan. Wouldn't it be great to live in it? But as long as that isn't possible, creating and looking at this cutie is a little consolation.

TOOLS & MATERIALS	THREAD COLOR GUIDE
» Stranded cotton embroidery thread » Embroidery needles » 5-inch embroidery hoop » White cotton fabric » Embroidery and fabric scissors	● DMC 152 Medium Light Shell Pink ● DMC 160 Medium Gray Blue ● DMC 420 Dark Hazelnut Brown ○ DMC 543 Ultra Very Light Beige ● DMC 729 Medium Old Gold ● DMC 924 Very Dark Gray Green ○ DMC 945 Tawny ● DMC 3771 Ultra Very Light Terra Cotta ○ DMC 3779 Very Light Rosewood ○ DMC 3823 Ultra Pale Yellow ● DMC 3827 Pale Golden Brown ● DMC 3857 Dark Rosewood

PATTERN

Note: This pattern is to scale for a 5-inch hoop.

Step 1

Transfer your design to the fabric and place it in your hoop.

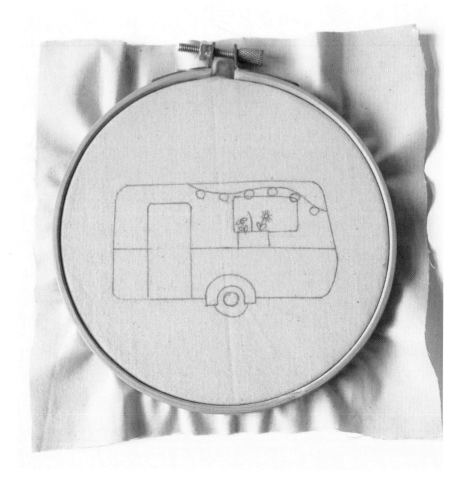

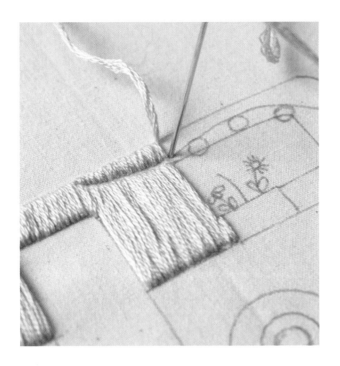

Step 2

Stitch the top and bottom of the caravan. Fill it with six strands and satin stitch, using DMC 945 (tawny) and 3771 (light terra cotta). Leave some space for the fairy lights. (You will fill this gap in step 6.) Make sure to stitch vertically from top to bottom or bottom to top. Don't stitch horizontally from left to right: the stitches would be too long and get loose.

Step 3

Stitch the wheel with six strands and satin stitch, going from the outside of the wheel to the inside. You will use DMC 152 (light pink), 3779 (light rosewood), and 543 (beige).

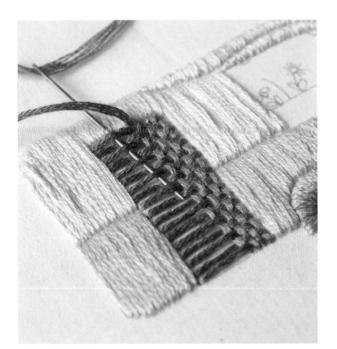

Step 4

Now you can add the doors and the little plant pot using DMC 420 (dark brown). Stitch it with weave stitch and full six strands. Do the horizontal lines first and then weave vertically from top to bottom, going over and under every other stitch.

Step 5

For the flowers, you need only two strands and three different stitches: whipped backstitch for the stems; satin stitch for the blossoms, the little leaves, and the center of the sunflower; and the French knot stitch for the lavender dots and the center of the daisy. Use only one turn for the French knot so the knots are really tiny. The colors used in this step are DMC 924 (dark gray green), 729 (medium old gold), 160 (medium gray blue), 3827 (pale golden brown), and 3857 (dark rosewood).

Step 6

Fill the gap you left in step 2 with a whipped backstitch and six strands. Use DMC 3779 (light rosewood).

Step 7

Now use six strands and French knot stitch for the lightbulbs. Use DMC 3823 (pale yellow) and do four turns for each French knot so the lightbulbs will be a little bit bigger. Make six or seven lightbulbs.

Step 8

Now you can finish your hoop by removing any visible lines following the instructions on your transfer pen. Attach your fabric to the hoop.

THERESA WENSING

Mushrooms

If you've embroidered enough flower meadows, try a cute little mushroom meadow! For this project, you only need three different stitches: satin stitch, French knot stitch, and reverse chain stitch. Sounds easy, right?

TOOLS & MATERIALS	THREAD COLOR GUIDE
» Stranded cotton embroidery thread » Embroidery needles » 6-inch oval embroidery hoop » White cotton fabric » Embroidery and fabric scissors	○ DMC 01 White Tin ○ DMC 20 Shrimp ○ DMC 25 Ultra Light Lavender ● DMC 30 Medium Light Blueberry ○ DMC 159 Light Gray Blue ○ DMC 225 Ultra Very Light Shell Pink ● DMC 316 Medium Antique Mauve ● DMC 498 Dark Red ● DMC 3727 Light Antique Mauve ○ DMC 3823 Ultra Pale Yellow

PATTERN

Note: This pattern is to scale for a 6-inch hoop.

Step 1

Transfer the design to your fabric and put the fabric into an oval hoop.

Step 2

Stitch the white stems with six strands of DMC 01 (white). Stitch the third from left (shown) and the right mushroom with a vertical satin stitch. Use a horizontal satin stitch for all other stems.

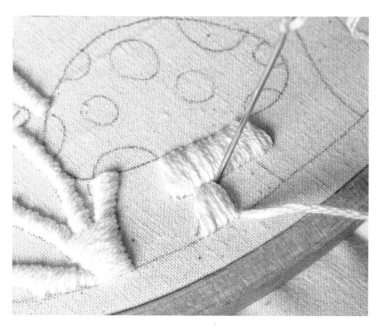

Step 3

Stitch the red fly agarics with the full six strands of DMC 498 (dark red) and 01 (white). Use a French knot stitch and one turn.

Step 4

Stitch the lower parts of these mushroom caps with a horizontal satin stitch. Use six strands and DMC 20 (shrimp).

Step 5

Stitch the upper part of these mushrooms with DMC 3823 (pale yellow) and a vertical satin stitch.

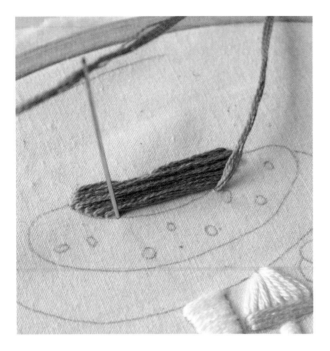

Step 6

Stitch the upper part of this mushroom with a horizontal satin stitch. Use six strands of DMC 316 (medium mauve).

Step 7

Stitch the middle part with a vertical satin stitch. Use DMC 3727 (light mauve) and six strands.

Step 8

Use six strands of DMC 225 (light pink) and a reverse satin stitch for the lower part. You can also use satin stitch if you want to avoid extra work.

Step 9

Finish this mushroom by adding some French knots above the middle part. Use six strands of DMC 01 (white). Do one turn so the French knots won't turn out too big.

Step 10

Stitch this mushroom like the mushroom in steps 6–9, with the following changes: Stitch the lower part with satin stitch instead of chain stitch. Use just three instead of six strands for the French knots so they will be smaller. Use DMC 30 (light blue), 159 (light gray blue), 25 (light lavender), and 01 (white) as pictured.

Remove any visible lines according to the instructions on your transfer pen and attach the fabric to the hoop.

THERESA WENSING

Flowers in Hand

Instead of gifting real flowers, try these little stitched ones. They will stay beautiful and timeless forever, no water or attention needed. And the best thing is that creating them is pretty easy—you just need five basic stitches.

TOOLS & MATERIALS	THREAD COLOR GUIDE
» Stranded cotton embroidery thread	● DMC 310 Black
» Embroidery needles	● DMC 341 Light Blue Violet
» 6-inch embroidery hoop	○ DMC 543 Ultra Very Light Beige
» White cotton fabric	● DMC 3689 Light Mauve
» Embroidery and fabric scissors	● DMC 3771 Ultra Very Light Terra Cotta
	● DMC 3813 Light Blue Green
	● DMC 3827 Pale Golden Brown

PATTERN

Note: This pattern is to scale for a 6-inch hoop.

Step 1

Transfer your design to the fabric and place it in a 6-inch hoop. You can choose whatever color you like for the fabric, but the flowers pop the most on plain white or cream.

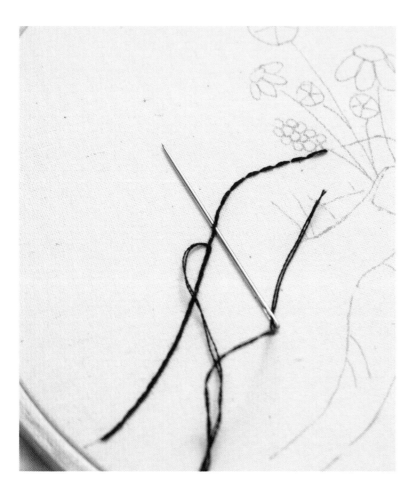

Step 2

Stitch the hand and the flower stems with a whipped backstitch, using DMC 310 (black) and 3813 (light blue green). Use two strands for the black outline and three strands for the green stems.

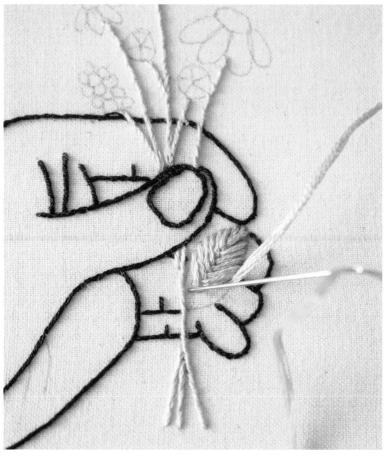

Step 3

Now stitch the leaf with a fishbone stitch with the same color as the stems. Use the full six strands.

Step 4

Stitch the center of the daises and the lavender blossoms with French knots. Use one turn for the orange knots (DMC 3827) and two turns for the purple knots (DMC 341).

Step 5

Now stitch the blossoms of the daisies with satin stitch and DMC 543 (light beige). Use the full six strands. You will need five to seven satin stitches per blossom.

Step 6

Finish the design by stitching all three circles with woven wheels. Use six strands for each circle so the roses pop out. Use DMC 3771 (light terra cotta) and 3689 (light mauve).

It's a bit tricky to stitch a really small woven wheel with six strands, so if you don't feel comfortable with it, you can use three strands instead.

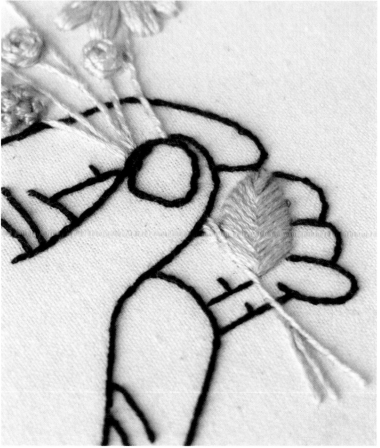

Step 7

Finish your hoop by removing the still-visible lines following the instructions on your transfer pen. Finish your hoop.

SOPHIE TIMMS

Floral Stick & Stitch

Anything looks better when it's embroidered with cute floral designs. Customize a hat, a tote bag, or even clothing with this project.

TOOLS & MATERIALS

- » Stranded cotton embroidery thread
- » Embroidery and fabric scissors
- » Embroidery needles
- » Water-soluble transfer stabilizer
- » Printer for printing the pattern onto the stabilizer
- » 4-inch embroidery hoop
- » Baseball cap or other surface to embroider on (see page 103)

THREAD COLOR GUIDE

- ○ DMC 3774 Very Light Desert Sand
- ○ DMC 224 Very Light Shell Pink
- ● DMC 223 Light Shell Pink
- ● DMC 436 Tan
- ○ DMC 3024 Very Light Brown Gray
- ● DMC 523 Light Fern Green
- ○ DMC 928 Very Light Gray Green
- ● DMC 926 Medium Gray Green

PATTERN

Note: Patterns aren't to scale and may need to be sized up for tracing. You can increase their size before embroidering.

Step 1

Print the designs onto your stabilizer. I like to use Sulky Fabric-Like Water Soluble Stabilizer. Once printed, cut around the outside of each design, leaving about a ⅓-inch gap.

Step 2

Decide how you want the designs arranged on the hat and stick each one down in place.

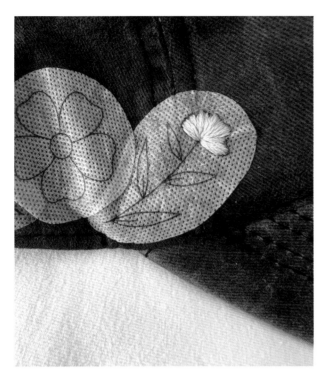

Step 3

Using three strands of satin stitch, fill the flowers with either light pink or dark blue, depending on which flower you are starting with. Use one strand of either rose pink or light blue and a straight stitch, and add more detail to the petals, with each stitch ending at the base of the petal.

Step 4

To finish these flowers off, use two strands of dark green backstitch and two strands of light green fishbone stitch to complete the leaves.

Step 5

Use three strands of either yellow or rose pink to fill the flowers using satin stitch. With three strands of either light or dark pink, use straight stitches to add detail to each petal, with each stitch ending at the center.

Embroidery is a great way of giving a new lease on life to your clothes, and it provides the opportunity to be mindful in the process!

Step 6

Fill the centers of the flowers with French knots wound twice in either yellow or dark pink.

Step 7

Using three strands of dark green and a fishbone stitch, fill in the leaves. Use one strand of light green and a backstitch to complete the stem.

Step 8

Once you've finished your stitches, wash off the stabilizer with warm water and let the hat dry.

SUGGESTIONS

HERE ARE SUGGESTIONS
FOR A COUPLE OF OTHER
ITEMS YOU COULD
EMBROIDER, AS WELL
AS INSPIRATION FOR
DESIGNS.

SOPHIE TIMMS

Floral Wreath

Embroidery is one of the most relaxing hobbies. One of my best tips is to stop doubting yourself and start the project you've been putting off. You'll be happy you did!

TOOLS & MATERIALS

- » Stranded cotton embroidery thread
- » Embroidery and fabric scissors
- » Embroidery needles
- » 6-inch embroidery hoop
- » Calico fabric: 2 layers, sized approximately 8" x 8"
- » Pilot FriXion heat-erasable pen (or your preferred method of pattern transfer)

THREAD COLOR GUIDE

- DMC 224 Very Light Shell Pink
- DMC 436 Tan
- DMC 522 Fern Green
- DMC 543 Ultra Very Light Beige
- DMC 926 Medium Gray Green
- DMC 928 Very Light Gray Green
- DMC 3859 Light Rosewood

PATTERN

Note: This pattern is to scale for a 6-inch hoop.

Step 1

Transfer the pattern onto your chosen fabric (see page 100).

Step 2

Using four strands of light green thread (DMC 928), fill the flower one petal at a time using satin stitch.

Step 3

Using six strands of rose pink thread (DMC 3859), fill the flower one petal at a time using satin stitch.

Mindfulness and creativity are intertwined. Take the time to create your own floral wreath to hang up in your home.

Step 4

To finish these flowers off, use three strands of tan thread (DMC 436) to fill in the flower centers. Each French knot is wound twice.

Step 5

Using three strands of light green (DMC 522), fill the leaves using the fishbone stitch. For the beige leaves, do the same again using the beige thread (DMC 543).

Step 6

Use two strands of the light green thread (DMC 522) and stem stitch to create the stems from the flowers and leaves.

Step 7

Fill in the small flowers using three strands of gray green (DMC 926) and satin stitch.

Step 8

Use one strand of light green (DMC 928) and straight stitch to complete the highlights on each flower. Add four to five small straight stitches ending at the base of the flower.

Step 9

With three strands of either light pink or rose pink (DMC 224 or 3859), wind the thread three times around the needle to create a chunkier knot.

Step 10

One half of the pattern is now complete! Duplicate the pattern on the other side of the hoop. Alternatively, you could just embroider one half, or add in a custom initial, name, or phrase in the center. Finish your hoop.

SOPHIE TIMMS

Wildflower Bouquet

Don't wait to be gifted a beautiful bouquet of flowers;
embroider your own everlasting flowers instead!

TOOLS & MATERIALS	THREAD COLOR GUIDE

TOOLS & MATERIALS

- » Stranded cotton embroidery thread
- » Embroidery and fabric scissors
- » Embroidery needles
- » 6-inch embroidery hoop
- » Calico fabric: 2 layers, sized approximately 8" x 8"
- » Pilot FriXion heat-erasable pen (or your preferred method of **pattern transfer**)

THREAD COLOR GUIDE

- ● DMC 167 Very Dark Yellow Beige
- ○ DMC 224 Very Light Shell Pink
- ● DMC 500 Very Dark Blue Green
- ● DMC 502 Blue Green
- ● DMC 729 Medium Old Gold
- ○ DMC 950 Light Desert Sand
- ● DMC 3726 Dark Antique Mauve
- ● DMC 3862 Dark Mocha Beige
- ● DMC 3864 Light Mocha Beige
- ○ DMC 3866 Ultra Very Light Mocha

PATTERN

Note: This pattern is to scale for a 6-inch hoop.

Step 1

Transfer the pattern onto your chosen fabric.

Step 2

Using six strands of yellow thread (DMC 729), fill the flower one petal at a time using satin stitch. Repeat for each of the yellow flowers.

Step 3

Using four strands of white thread (DMC 3866), fill each daisy one petal at a time using satin stitch.

Step 4

To finish these flowers off, use three strands of dark yellow (DMC 167) to fill in the flower center. Wind each French knot twice.

Step 5

Using three strands of light pink (DMC 950), fill the flowers one petal at a time using satin stitch.

Step 6

Use three strands of the dark yellow thread (DMC 167) and the French knot to create one knot at the center of each flower. Wind once to create a smaller, more delicate knot.

Step 7

Using two strands of dark pink (DMC 3726) and two strands of rose pink (DMC 224) to create four strands in total, create one French knot per "bubble" of the flower. To ensure they are large enough, wind the thread around the needle two to four times for each knot.

Taking a walk in nature can be all the inspiration you need. Why not stop and look at the flowers that you see and create a wildflower bouquet for yourself?

Step 8

Use four strands of light green (DMC 502) and satin stitch to complete one half of each leaf, ensuring the direction of the satin stitch is toward the center of the leaf. Do the same again using the dark green thread (DMC 500) for the other half of the leaf.

Step 9

With six strands of either light green or dark green (DMC 502 or 500), use the fishbone stitch to fill in each large leaf.

Step 10

To make the centers slightly raised, use the padded satin stitch. To do this, use six strands of dark brown thread (DMC 3862) and fill in the area with some seed stitches. Next, fill in each center with satin stitch in the usual way.

Step 11

Add in the detail to the large yellow flowers with one strand of dark yellow thread (DMC 167) and the straight stitch. Do this by adding in some long straight stitches in each petal that all end at the center of the flower.

Step 12

Fill in each flower with a collection of smaller French knots. Use three strands of light brown thread (DMC 3864) wound two or three times.

Step 13

Complete the pattern by finishing the stems to each element of the bouquet. Use two strands of light brown, light green, and dark green (DMC 3864, 502, and 500) and the stem stitch to do so. Finish the hoop.

SOPHIE TIMMS

Butterfly

Make like a butterfly and adapt and overcome! Test your embroidery skills with my two favorite stitches: satin stitch and the French knot!

TOOLS & MATERIALS

- » Stranded cotton embroidery thread
- » Embroidery and fabric scissors
- » Embroidery needles
- » 6-inch embroidery hoop
- » Calico fabric: 2 layers, sized approximately 8" x 8"
- » Robert Kauffman Essex Linen fabric in leather: 1 square, sized approximately 8" x 8"
- » Pilot FriXion heat-erasable pen (or your preferred method of pattern transfer)

THREAD COLOR GUIDE

- ● DMC 310 Black
- ● DMC 320 Medium Pistachio Green
- ● DMC 561 Very Dark Jade
- ● DMC 738 Very Light Tan
- ● DMC 920 Medium Copper
- ● DMC 977 Light Golden Brown
- ● DMC 3826 Golden Brown
- ○ DMC 3865 Winter White
- ○ DMC 3866 Ultra Very Light Mocha

PATTERN

Note: This pattern is to scale for a 6-inch hoop.

Step 1

Transfer the pattern onto your chosen fabric.

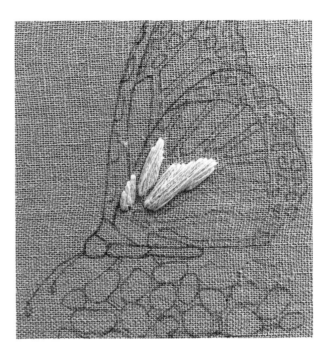

Step 2

Using six strands of light yellow thread (DMC 738), fill the sections of the wing using satin stitch. The direction of the satin stitches should point inward, toward the butterfly's body.

Step 3

Using six strands of pale orange thread (DMC 977), fill the sections of the wing using satin stitch.

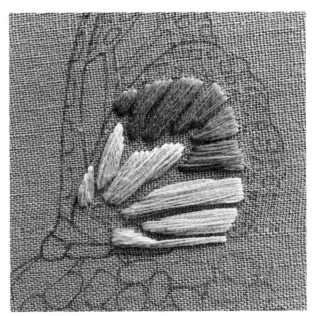

Step 4

To finish the lower wing, use six strands of dark orange thread (DMC 3826) to fill in the last six sections.

Step 5

Using six strands of the same dark orange (DMC 3826), fill the three sections at the top of the wing using satin stitch.

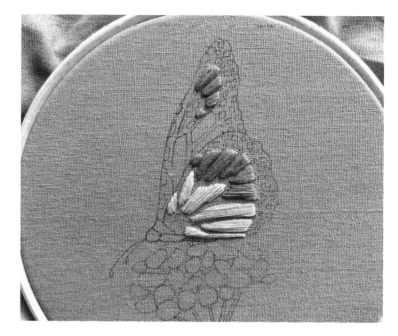

Step 6

Use six strands of red thread (DMC 920) and satin stitch to fill the middle of the upper wings.

Step 7

Using six strands of dark red and satin stitch, fill in the lower sections of the top wings.

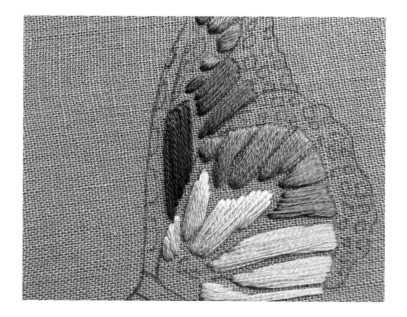

Step 8

Fill in the two small sections at the bottom of the lower wing using six strands of light yellow thread (DMC 738).

Spiritually, butterflies represent profound change and transformation. Accepting change is the epitome of mindfulness, so why not embroider a butterfly of your own?

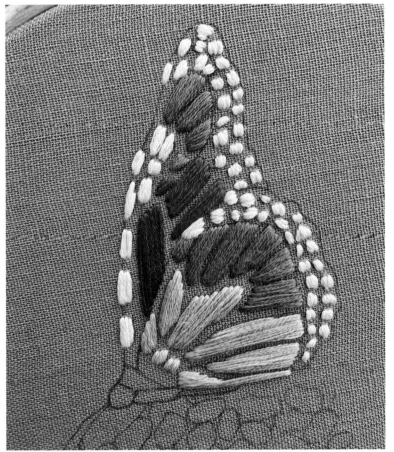

Step 9

With six strands of white thread (DMC 3865), use satin stitch to complete the small sections on the edges of each wing. Although the areas to fill are small, using six strands helps create more texture over and above the black parts of the wing.

Step 10

Using four strands of black thread (DMC 310), use satin stitch to fill in each segment of the body.

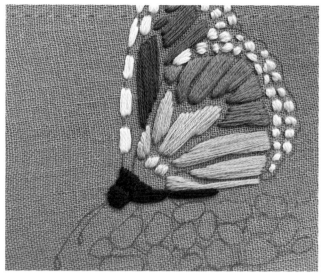

Step 11

Complete the wings by using two strands of black (DMC 310) to fill in with two long and short stitch.

Step 12

With one strand of black thread (DMC 310) and backstitch, stitch along the lines to complete the antennae and legs.

Step 13

Using three strands of beige (DMC 3866), fill in each section of the flower with individual French knots. Go around the edge of each section, winding each French knot twice to create even knots. Then fill in each section with more French knots until all sections are complete.

Step 14

Combine two strands of light green (DMC 320) and two strands of dark green (DMC 561) for four strands of thread, and then use long and short stitch to fill in the stem. Finish the hoop.

SOPHIE TIMMS

Floral Border on a Pillowcase

To me, the colors in this piece evoke feelings of coziness and calm—perfect for a pillow in a favorite room of your home.

TOOLS & MATERIALS

- » Embroidery needles
- » 6-inch embroidery hoop
- » Pillowcase in the size and color of your choice
- » Pilot FriXion heat-erasable pen (or your preferred method of pattern transfer)
- » Stranded cotton embroidery thread
- » Embroidery and fabric scissors

THREAD COLOR GUIDE

- DMC 372 Light Mustard
- DMC 436 Tan
- DMC 632 Ultra Very Dark Desert Sand
- DMC 3779 Very Light Rosewood
- DMC 3787 Dark Brown Gray
- DMC 3864 Light Mocha Beige
- DMC 3866 Ultra Very Light Mocha

PATTERN

Note: Patterns aren't to scale and may need to be sized up for tracing. You can print and increase their size before embroidering.

Step 1

Transfer the pattern onto your chosen fabric. Repeat the section of the pattern as required for the length of the pillowcase (or tea towel or whatever it is you choose to embroider).

Step 2

Using three strands of white (DMC 3866), fill the sections of the wing using the long and short stitch. The direction of the stitch should point inward toward the center of the flower. Due to the size of this flower and the fact that a pillowcase is likely to be washed regularly, long and short stitch will be more durable than satin stitch.

Step 3

Using three strands of yellow (DMC 436), fill the center of the flower with French knots, winding the thread twice for each.

Step 4

For each small flower, use three strands of brown (DMC 3864) to create each petal. Do this three times for each flower using satin stitch.

Step 5

Using three strands of burgundy (DMC 632), create each flower with French knots, winding the thread three times for each. The easiest method is to complete the outer circle first and then fill in the middle.

Step 6

Use six strands of light green (DMC 372) and fishbone stitch to fill the small leaves attached to each French knot flower.

Step 7

Using six strands of dark green (DMC 3787) and fishbone stitch, fill in the large leaf.

Step 8

Similar to step 2 with the white flower, use three strands of coral (DMC 3779) to fill in each petal of the coral flowers with the long and short stitch. Rather than stitching all the way to the line, leave an uneven edge so you can blend in the next section.

Step 9

With three strands of brown (DMC 3864), use the long and short stitch to complete the small sections at the base of each petal. Blend in the uneven edge of the coral thread.

Step 10

Using three strands of yellow (DMC 436), use the French knot wound three times to fill in the center.

Step 11

Use six strands of brown (DMC 3864) and the lazy daisy stitch to create each petal, similar to step 4.

Step 12

With the same six strands of brown, use straight stitch to fill in each petal.

Step 13

Using three strands of burgundy (DMC 632), fill in each section of the flower with satin stitch. Try to fill in each petal horizontally so the petals can be distinguished from each other.

Rest a little easier each night with a beautifully embroidered pillowcase.

Step 14

Fill in the centers of these flowers with French knots, using three strands of yellow (DMC 436) and winding the thread twice for each French knot. Use three strands of DMC 3787 and satin stitch to fill in the small stem section at the base of the flower. Backstitch for the stem.

Step 15

Use three strands of yellow (DMC 436) and satin stitch to fill in each petal on the yellow flower.

Step 16

As with previous flower centers, fill in the center of the flower with French knots. Use three strands of brown (DMC 3864) and wind three times.

Step 17

As with step 7, fill in the leaf with six strands of fishbone stitch, using light green (DMC 372).

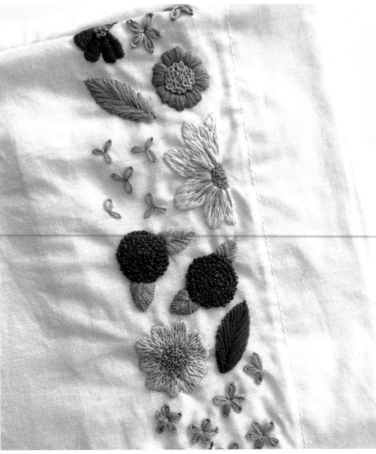

Step 18

One complete section of the pattern is now finished. Repeat the pattern as required depending on how big your fabric is. This pattern is not limited to pillowcase edging and could be used for a tea towel, the hem of a skirt, dress, or sleeve, a tote bag, and more!

SOPHIE TIMMS

Detailed Flower Outline

Sometimes, the detail is in the simplicity! Practice your backstitch with this project using a colorful fabric of your choice. I've used black thread on pink fabric, but you can use any color combination you like.

TOOLS & MATERIALS	THREAD COLOR GUIDE
» Stranded cotton embroidery thread	● DMC 310 Black
» Embroidery and fabric scissors	
» Embroidery needles	
» 6-inch embroidery hoop	
» Calico fabric: 2 layers, sized approximately 8" x 8"	
» Robert Kauffman Essex Linen fabric in peach: 1 square, sized approximately 8" x 8"	
» Pilot FriXion heat-erasable pen (or your preferred method of pattern transfer)	

PATTERN

Note: This pattern is to scale for a 6-inch hoop.

Step 1

Transfer the pattern to your chosen fabric. Due to the nature of the outline pattern, this one looks lovely on colored fabric.

Sometimes, stopping and smelling the roses can make your day just that little bit better.

Step 2

Using two strands of black thread (DMC 310), follow the flower outline one petal at a time using backstitch.

Step 3

Continue with the backstitch until the entire outline is completed.

Step 4

Using two strands of black thread, backstitch the outlines of the leaves.

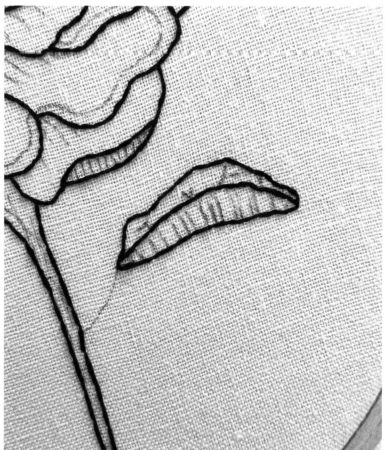

Step 5

For the smaller details on the leaves, use just one strand of black thread and backstitch.

Step 6

Use one strand of black to back-stitch the small details of the large flower, working on each petal until the flower is completed.

About the Artists

JENNY BILLINGHAM is a self-taught embroidery artist from the United Kingdom. In 2020, she began experimenting with simple stitches and embroidery designs. Since then, she has created hoop art and embroidery patterns, and it has become far more than just a hobby. Jenny has always been a craft enthusiast and loved studying surface design and printed textiles at the University of Northampton. Her embroidery designs feature texture and pattern, and she loves to keep things bold, colorful, and unique. Jenny's designs use a range of yarns, and she is often inspired by simple shapes and florals. Some of the most popular designs she has created have been her stars and hearts, and more recently embroidered clothing. Jenny's main focus is to encourage upcycling and the rejuvenation of garments, especially denim items and sweatshirts. Jenny absolutely loves embroidery and has found it very exciting to see how popular it has become in recent years.

THERESA WENSING is an embroidery artist from Germany. She started embroidering two years ago, when scrolling through social media and watching TV stopped entertaining her. She taught herself the traditional craft of embroidery and gave it a modern touch with her cute designs.

SOPHIE TIMMS is a self-taught embroidery artist based in the United Kingdom. Having always been a creative soul, she learned how to embroider so that during times of uncertainty, she could keep her hands busy and mind at rest. Thanks to its therapeutic and relaxing nature, embroidery very quickly became, and remains to this day, her comfort. Seeking inspiration in nature and mindfulness, Sophie finds so much joy in creating embroidery projects and patterns from start to finish so that others can learn the craft too. Sophie's embroideries are often focused on floral arrangements and muted colors, evoking coziness and calm through her art.